Collins
First
French
Dictionary

Published by Collins

An imprint of HarperCollins Publishers
Westerhill Road
Bishopbriggs
Glasgow G64 2QT

Third Edition 2020

Published as *Collins Very First French Dictionary*
2009, 2014

10 9 8 7 6 5 4 3 2 1

Text © HarperCollins Publishers 2009, 2014, 2020
Illustrations © Maria Herbert-Liew 2020

ISBN 978-0-00-831271-8

www.schools.collinsdictionary.com
www.collins.co.uk/dictionaries

Typeset by QBS Learning

Printed and bound in the UK by Martins the Printer Ltd

A catalogue record for this book is available from the British Library.

If you would like to comment on any aspect of this book, please contact us at the given address or e-mail
dictionaries@harpercollins.co.uk.

Acknowledgements

We would like to thank those authors and publishers who kindly gave permission for copyright material to be used in the Collins Corpus. We would also like to thank Times Newspapers Ltd for providing valuable data.

Managing Editor:
Maree Airlie

Artwork and Design:
Maria Herbert-Liew

For the Publisher:
Kerry Ferguson
Michelle I'Anson

Audio pronunciation for every French word and sentence at collins.co.uk/homeworkhelp.

Contents

How to use your dictionary   5

Word classes   6

Colours
Les couleurs   9

Shapes
Les formes   9

Numbers
Les nombres   10

The days of the week
Les jours de la semaine   11

The months of the year
Les mois de l'année   11

Seasons
Les saisons   12

The weather
Le temps   13

Dictionary A to Z   **14**

Conversations
Les conversations   56

Things I like to do
Les choses que j'aime faire   58

The park
Le parc   60

The seaside   61
Le bord de mer

Vehicles   62
Les véhicules

Food and drink   64
La nourriture et les boissons

Clothes   66
Les vêtements

Parts of the body   67
Le corps

Family   68
La famille

Animals   70
Les animaux

Wild animals   72
Les animaux sauvages

Mythical creatures   74
Les créatures légendaires

French-English Index   **75**

How to use your dictionary

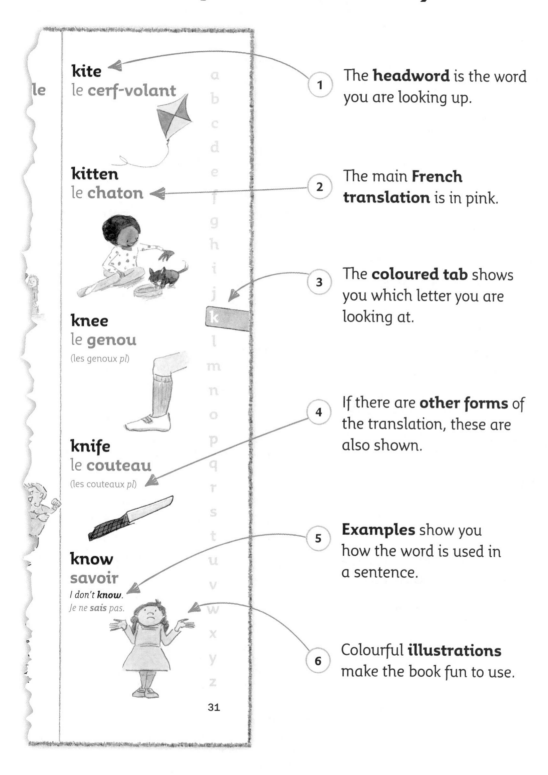

kite
le **cerf-volant**

1. The **headword** is the word you are looking up.

kitten
le **chaton**

2. The main **French translation** is in pink.

3. The **coloured tab** shows you which letter you are looking at.

knee
le **genou**
(les genoux *pl*)

knife
le **couteau**
(les couteaux *pl*)

4. If there are **other forms** of the translation, these are also shown.

5. **Examples** show you how the word is used in a sentence.

know
savoir
*I don't **know**.*
*Je ne **sais** pas.*

6. Colourful **illustrations** make the book fun to use.

31

le

a b c d e f g h i j k l m n o p q r s t u v w x y z

Word classes

Nouns

A **noun** is a word that is used for talking about a person or thing. **Nouns** are sometimes called "naming words" because they are often the names of people, places and things, for example:

> **man** *noun*
> **park** *noun*
> **bird** *noun*
> **computer** *noun*

Nouns are very often found after the words *a* and *the* or words like *our*, *my* or *his*.

We watched a <u>cartoon</u> on the <u>laptop</u>.
My <u>brother</u> is playing in the <u>park</u>.

Proper nouns are the names of people, places, days and months and <u>always</u> start with a capital letter.

> **Emma** *noun*
> **London** *noun*
> **Friday** *noun*
> **June** *noun*

<u>John</u> lives in <u>Glasgow</u>.
He went home on <u>Friday</u>.

When a **noun** is used with another word or words, this can be called a **noun phrase**.

She was wearing <u>a beautiful red dress</u>.
<u>All the children</u> were sleeping.

Some French nouns are:

la **pomme** (meaning *apple*)
le **cheval** (meaning *horse*)
l'**insecte** (meaning *insect*)
l'**amie** *f* (meaning *friend*)

La bouteille est <u>vide</u>.
(meaning *The bottle is empty*.)

In French, nouns can be *masculine* (*m*) or *feminine* (*f*). This is shown by *le* or *la* in front of the noun.

la **pomme** → <u>la</u> shows that it's a *feminine* noun
le **cheval** → <u>le</u> shows that it's a *masculine* noun

Nouns which have *l'* in front of them can be either *masculine* or *feminine*. The abbreviation after the noun tells you which one it is.

l'**insecte** *m* → *m* tells you that this a *masculine* noun
l'**amie** *f* → *f* tells you that this is a *feminine* noun

If the French word has *les* in front of it, this means that the word is plural (there is more than one of it).
les **feux d'artifice** *mpl* (meaning *fireworks*)

Verbs

A **verb** is a word that you use for saying what someone or something does. **Verbs** are often called "doing words" because they talk about an action that someone or something is doing, for example:

eat *verb*
cry *verb*
talk *verb*

Verbs are often found after nouns, or words like *she*, *they* or *it*.

The dog barks at the cat.
She eats sandwiches for lunch.

When you want to talk about something that you are doing right now (in the present), you use the **present tense** of the verb.

The children are talking to each other.
She does her homework before dinner.

When you want to talk about something that you did earlier (in the past), you use the **past tense** of the verb.

Anna cried when she fell off her bike.
The beetle ran across the floor.

You can make the **past tense** of many verbs by adding *d* or *ed* to the end of the verb, for example:

walk → *walked*
dance → *danced*

Sometimes you need to double the last letter before adding the *ed* ending in the **past tense**, for example:

stop → *stopped*
hug → *hugged*

Some verbs have a completely different way of making the **past tense**, for example:

go → *went*
sing → *sang*

Some French verbs are:

donner (meaning *give*)
aimer (meaning *like*)
trouver (meaning *find*)

Donne-moi le livre, s'il te plaît.
(meaning *Give me the book, please.*)

Je ne trouve plus mes bottes.
(meaning *I can't find my boots.*)

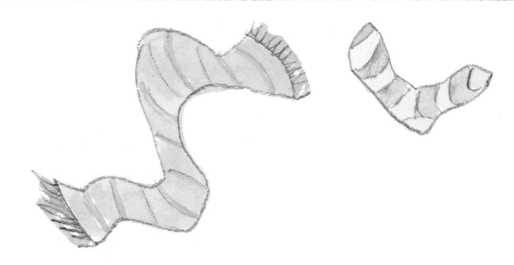

Adjectives

An **adjective** is a word that tells you more about a person or thing. **Adjectives** are often called "describing words" because they describe what something looks, feels, or smells like, for example:

> **big** *adjective*
> **soft** *adjective*
> **nice** *adjective*

Adjectives are very often found before a noun, or after the verb *to be*.
She lives in a <u>big</u> house.
The caterpillar is <u>long</u> and <u>green</u>.

When you want to talk about something that is more than something else, you can use an **adjective** in different forms, usually ending in *er* or *est*.

bigger, biggest
soft, softer
nicer, nicest

I have the <u>nicest</u> sister in the world!
Yesterday was the <u>wettest</u> day of the year.

Some French adjectives are:

bon (meaning *good*)
gentil (meaning *kind*)
facile (meaning *easy*)

Elle est <u>heureuse</u>.
(meaning *She's happy*.)

In French, adjectives can change depending on whether the noun they describe is *masculine* or *feminine*.

le <u>bon</u> film
(meaning *the good film*)

la <u>bonne</u> idée
(meaning *the good idea*)

le garçon <u>gentil</u>
(meaning *the kind boy*)

la fille <u>gentille</u>
(meaning *the kind girl*)

Adverbs

An **adverb** is a word that tells you more about how someone does something, for example:

> **happily** *adverb*
> **slowly** *adverb*
> **well** *adverb*

Adverbs are very often found after verbs, or sometimes before adjectives.

The snail moved <u>slowly</u> along the path.
The game was <u>really</u> exciting!

An example of a French adverb is:

vite (meaning *fast*)

Elles peuvent courir <u>vite</u>.
(meaning *They can run fast*.)

Colours
Les couleurs

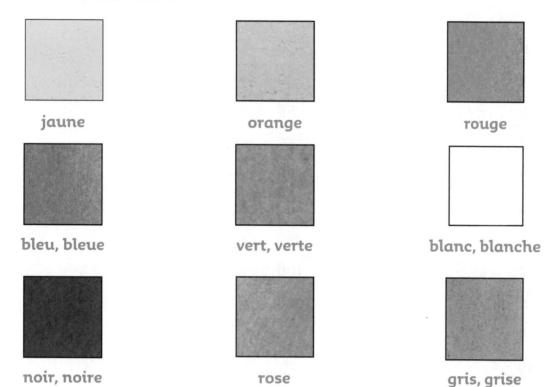

jaune

orange

rouge

bleu, bleue

vert, verte

blanc, blanche

noir, noire

rose

gris, grise

Shapes
Les formes

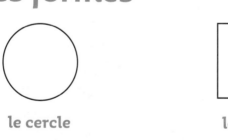

le cercle

le carré

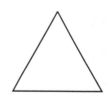

le triangle

le rectangle

l'étoile *f*

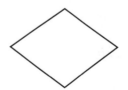

le losange

Numbers
Les nombres

0	zéro		30	trente
1	un		40	quarante
2	deux		50	cinquante
3	trois		60	soixante
4	quatre		70	soixante-dix
5	cinq		80	quatre-vingts
6	six		90	quatre-vingt-dix
7	sept		100	cent
8	huit		1000	mille
9	neuf			
10	dix			
11	onze			
12	douze			
13	treize			
14	quatorze			
15	quinze			
16	seize			
17	dix-sept			
18	dix-huit			
19	dix-neuf			
20	vingt			

The days of the week
Les jours de la semaine

Monday	lundi
Tuesday	mardi
Wednesday	mercredi
Thursday	jeudi
Friday	vendredi
Saturday	samedi
Sunday	dimanche

The months of the year
Les mois de l'année

January	janvier
February	février
March	mars
April	avril
May	mai
June	juin
July	juillet
August	août
September	septembre
October	octobre
November	novembre
Decembe	décembre

Seasons
Les saisons

spring
le printemps

summer
l'été *m*

autumn
l'automne *m*

winter
l'hiver *m*

The weather
Le temps

It's cloudy. Il fait gris.

It's hot. Il fait chaud.

It's raining. Il pleut.

It's windy. Il y a du vent.

It's snowing. Il neige.

It's cold. Il fait froid.

again
encore une fois

*Try **again**!*
*Essaie **encore une fois** !*

animal
l'**animal** *m*

(les animaux *pl*)

adult
l'**adulte** *m/f*

app
l'**appli** *f*

alphabet
l'**alphabet** *m*

aeroplane
l'**avion** *m*

apple
la **pomme**

after
après

after lunch
après le déjeuner

ambulance
l'**ambulance** *f*

arm
le **bras**

and
et

*my cat **and** me*
*mon chat **et** moi*

ask
demander à

***Ask** somebody.*
***Demande à** quelqu'un.*

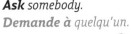

afternoon
l'**après-midi** *m*

*at four o'clock in the **afternoon***
à quatre heures de
l'après-midi

baby
le **bébé**

bad
mauvais,
mauvaise

bad weather
le *mauvais* temps

bag
le **sac**

ball
le **ballon**

balloon
le **ballon**

banana
la **banane**

basket
le **panier**

bath
le **bain**

beach
la **plage**

bed
le **lit**

bedroom
la **chambre**

before
avant

before three o'clock
avant trois heures

bicycle
le **vélo**

a
b
c
d
e
f
g
h
i
j
k
l
m
n
o
p
q
r
s
t
u
v
w
x
y
z

big
grand, grande
*a **big** house*
*une **grande** maison*

bird
l'**oiseau** m
(les oiseaux *pl*)

birthday
l'**anniversaire** m
*Happy **birthday**!*
*Joyeux **anniversaire** !*

black
noir, noire
*a **black** dog*
*un chien **noir***

blanket
la **couverture**

blue
bleu, bleue
*a **blue** dress*
*une robe **bleue***

boat
le **bateau**
(les bateaux *pl*)

body
le **corps**

book
le **livre**

boot
la **botte**

box
la **boîte**

boy
le **garçon**

bread
le **pain**

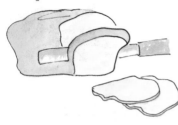

breakfast
le **petit déjeuner**

bridge
le **pont**

bring
apporter

*Could you **bring** me a glass of water?*
*Tu peux m'**apporter** un verre d'eau ?*

brother
le **frère**

bucket
le **seau**

(les seaux *pl*)

burger
le **hamburger**

bus
le **bus**

butter
le **beurre**

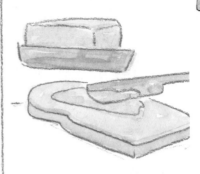

butterfly
le **papillon**

buy
acheter

*She's **buying** fruit.*
*Elle **achète** des fruits.*

a b **c** d e f g h i j k l m n o p q r s t u v w x y z

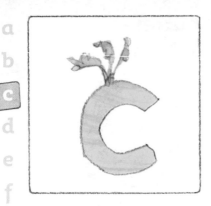

cake
le **gâteau**

(les gâteaux *pl*)

calendar
le **calendrier**

call
appeler

Call this number.
Appelle ce numéro.

candle
la **bougie**

cap
la **casquette**

car
la **voiture**

card
la **carte**

carrot
la **carotte**

castle
le **château**

(les châteaux *pl*)

cat
le **chat**

caterpillar
la **chenille**

chair
la **chaise**

cheese
le **fromage**

chicken
le **poulet**

child
l'**enfant** *m/f*

chips
les **frites** *fpl*

chocolate
le **chocolat**

chopsticks
les **baguettes** *fpl*

circle
le **cercle**

circus
le **cirque**

classroom
la **classe**

clean
propre
*a **clean** shirt*
*une chemise **propre***

clock
l'**horloge** *f*

clothes
les **vêtements** *mpl*

cloud
le **nuage**

clown
le **clown**

coat
le **manteau**
(les manteaux *pl*)

coffee
le **café**

cold
froid, froide
I'm **cold**.
*J'ai **froid**.*

come
venir
Come to me!
***Viens** à moi !*

computer
l'**ordinateur** *m*

cook
cuisiner
*I can **cook**.*
*Je sais **cuisiner**.*

costume
le **costume**

count
compter

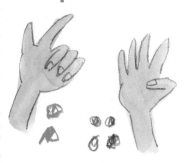

cow
la **vache**

cry
pleurer
*Why **are** you **crying**?*
*Pourquoi tu **pleures** ?*

cup
la **tasse**

d

dad
le **papa**

dance
danser

*I like **dancing**.*
*J'aime **danser**.*

dangerous
dangereux,
dangereuse

*It's **dangerous**!*
*C'est **dangereux** !*

daughter
la **fille**

day
le **jour**

*What **day** is it today?*
*Quel **jour** sommes-nous ?*

dessert
le **dessert**

dictionary
le **dictionnaire**

difficult
difficile

*It's **difficult**.*
*C'est **difficile**.*

dinner
le **dîner**

dinosaur
le **dinosaure**

dirty
sale

*The dishes are **dirty**.*
*La vaisselle est **sale**.*

do
faire

*What **are** you **doing**?*
*Qu'est-ce que tu **fais** ?*

doctor
le **médecin** *m/*
la **médecin** *f*

dog
le **chien**

doll
la **poupée**

dolphin
le **dauphin**

door
la **porte**

downstairs
en bas

I'm downstairs!
Je suis en bas !

draw
dessiner

dream
le **rêve**

dress
la **robe**

drink
boire

Drink *your water.*
Bois *ton eau.*

drum
le **tambour**

duck
le **canard**

DVD
le **DVD**

ear
l'**oreille** *f*

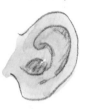

Earth
la **Terre**

easy
facile

*It's **easy**.*
*C'est **facile** !*

eat
manger

*I **eat** a lot of fruit.*
*Je **mange** beaucoup de fruits.*

egg
l'**œuf** *m*

elephant
l'**éléphant** *m*

email
le **mail**

empty
vide

*The bottle is **empty**.*
*La bouteille est **vide**.*

evening
le **soir**

*at six o'clock in the **evening**
à six heures du **soir***

every
tout, toute

(tous *pl*)
*I brush my teeth **every** day.*
*Je me brosse les dents **tous** les jours.*

exercise
l'**exercice** *m*

eye
l'**œil** *m*

(les yeux *pl*)

face
la **figure**

family
la **famille**

fast
vite

*They can run **fast**.*
*Elles peuvent courir **vite**.*

father
le **père**

---

favourite
préféré,
préférée

*Pink is my **favourite** colour.*
*Ma couleur **préférée**, c'est le rose.*

feather
la **plume**

find
trouver

*I can't **find** my boots.*
*Je ne **trouve** plus mes bottes.*

finger
le **doigt**

---

fire
le **feu**

(les feux *pl*)

fireworks
les **feux d'artifice** *mpl*

first
premier,
première

***first** prize*
*le **premier** prix*

fish
le **poisson**

floor
Sit on the **floor**.
Assieds-toi par terre.

flower
la **fleur**

fly
la **mouche**

food
la **nourriture**

football
le **football**

forest
la **forêt**

fork
la **fourchette**

fridge
le **frigo**

friend
l'**ami** *m*/l'**amie** *f*

frog
la **grenouille**

from
de
*a letter **from** my friend*
*une lettre **de** mon ami*

fruit
le **fruit**

full
plein, pleine
*The bottles are **full**.*
*Les bouteilles sont **pleines**.*

funny
drôle
*It's very **funny**.*
*C'est très **drôle**.*

game
le **jeu**

(les jeux *pl*)

garage
le **garage**

garden
le jardin

gate
le **portail**

giraffe
la **girafe**

girl
la **fille**

give
donner

Give me the book, please.
Donne-moi le livre, s'il te plaît.

glass
le **verre**

glasses
les **lunettes** *fpl*

glove
le **gant**

glue
la **colle**

go
aller

*Where **are** you **going**?*
*Où **vas**-tu ?*

goat
la **chèvre**

goldfish
le **poisson rouge**

good
bon, bonne

*That's a **good** idea.*
*C'est une **bonne** idée.*

goodbye
au revoir !

grapes
les **raisins** *mpl*

grass
l'**herbe** *f*

ground
la **terre**

*We sat on the **ground**.*
*Nous nous sommes assis par **terre**.*

grow
grandir

*Haven't you **grown**!*
*Comme tu as **grandi** !*

guinea pig
le **cochon d'Inde**

guitar
la **guitare**

hair
les **cheveux** mpl

She's got black **hair**.
*Elle a les **cheveux** noirs.*

hairdresser
le **coiffeur** m/
la **coiffeuse** f

hamster
le **hamster**

hand
la **main**

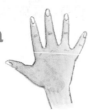

happy
heureux,
heureuse

She's **happy**.
*Elle est **heureuse**.*

hard
dur, dure

This cheese is very **hard**.
*Ce fromage est très **dur**.*

hat
le **chapeau**

(les chapeaux pl)

have
avoir

I **have** a bike.
*J'**ai** un vélo.*

head
la **tête**

hear
entendre

I can't **hear** you.
*Je ne t'**entends** pas.*

hedgehog
le **hérisson**

helicopter
l'**hélicoptère** m

hello
bonjour !

here
ici
*I live **here**.*
*J'habite **ici**.*

hide
se cacher
*They**'re hiding** behind the tree.*
*Ils **se cachent** derrière l'arbre.*

holiday
les vacances *fpl*
*We're on **holiday**.*
*Nous sommes en **vacances**.*

homework
les devoirs *mpl*

horse
le cheval
(les chevaux *pl*)

hospital
l'hôpital *m*
(les hôpitaux *pl*)

hot
chaud, chaude
*I'm **hot**.*
*J'ai **chaud**.*

hour
l'heure *f*

house
la maison

hug
serrer dans ses bras

hungry
I'm **hungry**.
*J'ai **faim**.*

hurry up
se dépêcher
***Hurry up**, children!*
***Dépêchez-vous**, les enfants !*

a b c d e f g **h** i j k l m n o p q r s t u v w x y z

ice cream
la **glace**

insect
l'**insecte** m

internet
l'**Internet** m

island
l'**île** f

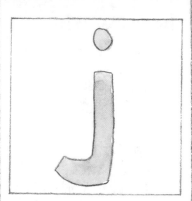

jacket
la **veste**

jam
la **confiture**

jeans
le **jean**

jigsaw
le **puzzle**

job
le **travail**

juice
le **jus**

*Don't spill your **juice**!*
*Ne renverse pas ton **jus** !*

jump
sauter

Jump!
Saute !

K

keep
garder

*You can **keep** the book.*
*Tu peux **garder** le livre.*

key
la **clé**

kid
le **gosse** *m/*
la **gosse** *f*

kind
gentil, gentille

*a **kind** person*
*une personne **gentille***

king
le **roi**

kiss
le **bisou**

*Give me a **kiss**.*
*Fais-moi un **bisou**.*

kitchen
la **cuisine**

kite
le **cerf-volant**

kitten
le **chaton**

knee
le **genou**

(les genoux pl)

knife
le **couteau**

(les couteaux pl)

know
savoir

*I don't **know**.*
*Je ne **sais** pas.*

a
b
c
d
e
f
g
h
i
j
k
l
m
n
o
p
q
r
s
t
u
v
w
x
y
z

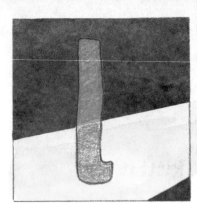

lamp
la **lampe**

learn
apprendre

*I'm **learning** to dance.*
*J'**apprends** à danser.*

lady
la **dame**

laptop
le **portable**

leg
la **jambe**

lemon
le **citron**

lake
le **lac**

late
en retard

*I'm **late** for school.*
*Je suis **en retard** pour l'école.*

less
moins

*I've got **less** than him!*
*J'en ai **moins** que lui !*

lamb
l'**agneau** *m*

(les agneaux *pl*)

laugh
rire

*Why **are** you **laughing**?*
*Pourquoi tu **ris** ?*

letter
la **lettre**

light
la **lumière**

like
aimer
*I **like** cherries.*
*J'**aime** les cerises.*

lion
le lion

listen
écouter
Listen to me!
Écoute-moi !

little
petit, petite
*a **little** girl*
*une **petite** fille*

live
habiter
*I **live** here.*
*J'**habite** ici.*

look
regarder
Look at the picture.
Regarde cette image.

lorry
le camion

lost
perdu, perdue
*I'm **lost**.*
*Je suis **perdue**.*

loud
fort, forte
*It's too **loud**.*
*C'est trop **fort**.*

love
aimer
*I **love** you.*
*Je t'**aime**.*

lucky
*You're **lucky**!*
*Tu as **de la chance** !*

lunch
le déjeuner

magician
le **magicien** *m*/
la **magicienne** *f*

make
faire

*I'm going to **make** a cake.*
*Je vais **faire** un gâteau.*

man
l'**homme** *m*

many
beaucoup de

*There are so **many** books!*
*Il y a **beaucoup de** livres !*

market
le **marché**

meal
le **repas**

meat
la **viande**

medicine
le **médicament**

meet
rencontrer

*I **met** my friend in town.*
*J'ai **rencontré** mon amie*
en ville.

mess
le **bazar**

milk
le **lait**

mobile
le **portable**

money
l'**argent** *m*

monkey
le **singe**

month
le **mois**

*What **month** is it?*
*Quel **mois** sommes-nous ?*

moon
la **lune**

more
plus de

*There are **more** girls than boys.*
*Il y a **plus de** filles que de garçons.*

morning
le **matin**

*at seven o'clock in the **morning***
*à sept heures du **matin***

mother
la **mère**

motorbike
la **moto**

mountain
la **montagne**

mouse
la **souris**

mouth
la **bouche**

mum
la **maman**

music
la **musique**

name
le **nom**

need
avoir besoin de

*I **need** a rubber.*
*J'**ai besoin d'**une gomme.*

neighbour
le **voisin** *m/*
la **voisine** *f*

new
nouveau,
nouvelle

*my **new** shoes*
*mes **nouvelles** chaussures*

newspaper
le **journal**

(les journaux *pl*)

next
prochain,
prochaine

*the **next** street on the left*
*la **prochaine** rue à gauche*

nice
gentil, gentille

*He's **nice**.*
*Il est **gentil**.*

night
la **nuit**

noise
le **bruit**

nose
le **nez**

(les nez *pl*)

now
maintenant

number
le **numéro**

nurse
l'**infirmier** *m/*
l'**infirmière** *f*

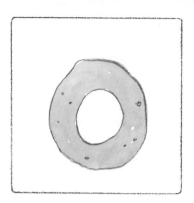

orange
l'**orange** *f*

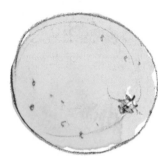

of
de

*the middle **of** the room*
*le milieu **de** la pièce*

other
autre

*on the **other** side of the table*
*de l'**autre** côté de la table*

old
vieux, vieille

*an **old** dog*
*un **vieux** chien*

open
ouvrir

*Why **did** you **open** the cage?*
*Pourquoi est-ce que tu **as** **ouvert** la cage ?*

page
la **page**

paint
peindre

*I'm going to **paint** them blue.*
*Je vais les **peindre** en bleu.*

paper
le **papier**

parents
les **parents** *mpl*

peas
les **petits pois** *mpl*

pet
l'**animal** *m*

(les animaux *pl*)

park
le **parc**

pen
le **stylo**

pencil
le **crayon**

phone
le **téléphone**

party
la **fête**

photo
la **photo**

people
les **gens** *mpl*

piano
le **piano**

pasta
les **pâtes** *fpl*

picnic
le **pique-nique**

picture
le **dessin**

pirate
le **pirate**

pizza
la **pizza**

plane
l'**avion** m

plant
la **plante**

play
jouer

I **play** tennis.
Je **joue** au tennis.

playground
l'**aire de jeux** f

pocket
la **poche**

pocket money
l'**argent
de poche** m

police officer
le **policier** m/
la **policière** f

pony
le **poney**

a
b
c
d
e
f
g
h
i
j
k
l
m
n
o
p
q
r
s
t
u
v
w
x
y
z

postcard
la **carte postale**

potato
la **pomme de terre**

present
le **cadeau**

(les cadeaux *pl*)

pretty
joli, jolie

*a **pretty** dress*
*une **jolie** robe*

prince
le **prince**

princess
la **princesse**

puddle
la **flaque**

puppet
la **marionnette**

puppy
le **chiot**

pushchair
la **poussette**

pyjamas
le **pyjama**

q

queen
la **reine**

quick
rapide
*a **quick** lunch*
*un déjeuner **rapide***

quiet
tranquille
*a **quiet** little town*
*une petite ville **tranquille***

r

rabbit
le **lapin**

race
la **course**

radio
la **radio**

rain
la **pluie**

rainbow
l'**arc-en-ciel** *m*

read
lire
*I **read** a lot.*
*Je **lis** beaucoup.*

ready
prêt, prête
*Breakfast is **ready**.*
*Le petit déjeuner est **prêt**.*

red
rouge
*a **red** jumper*
*un pull **rouge***

restaurant
le **restaurant**

ribbon
le **ruban**

rice
le **riz**

rich
riche

He's very **rich**.
Il est très **riche**.

right
bon, bonne

the **right** answer
la **bonne** réponse

ring
la **bague**

river
la **rivière**

road
la **route**

robot
le **robot**

rocket
la **fusée**

room
la **pièce**

run
courir

Run!
Cours !

sad
triste
*He's **sad**.*
*Il est **triste**.*

same
même
*They're in the **same** class.*
*Ils sont dans la **même** classe.*

sand
le **sable**

sandwich
le **sandwich**

say
dire
*What **did** you **say**?*
*Qu'est-ce que tu **as dit** ?*

scared
*I'm **scared**.*
*J'ai **peur**.*

school
l'**école** f

scissors
les **ciseaux** mpl

sea
la **mer**

second
deuxième

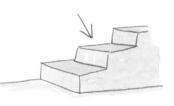

see
voir
*I can **see** myself in the water.*
*Je me **vois** dans l'eau.*

selfie
le **selfie**

a b c d e f g h i j k l m n o p q r **s** t u v w x y z

send
envoyer
Send me an email.
Envoie-moi un mail.

shadow
l'ombre f

sheep
le mouton

shirt
la chemise

shoe
la chaussure

shop
le magasin

shorts
le short

shout
crier
Don't shout!
Ne criez pas !

show
montrer
Show me the photos.
Montre-moi les photos.

shower
la douche

sick
malade
She is sick.
Elle est malade.

sing
chanter
I love to sing.
J'aime chanter.

sister
la sœur

sit
s'asseoir
*Can I **sit** here?*
*Je peux **m'asseoir** ici ?*

skin
la peau

skirt
la jupe

sky
le ciel

sleep
dormir
*My cat **sleeps** in a box.*
*Mon chat **dort** dans une boîte.*

slow
lent, lente
*The tortoise is very **slow**.*
*La tortue est très **lente**.*

smell
sentir
*Mmm, that **smells** good!*
*Mmm, ça **sent** bon !*

smile
le sourire

snail
l'escargot *m*

snake
le serpent

snow
la neige

snowman
le bonhomme de neige

soap
le savon

sock
la **chaussette**

sofa
le **canapé**

son
le **fils**

sorry
pardon !

soup
la **soupe**

space
l'**espace** *m*

speak
parler
*Do you **speak** English?*
*Est-ce que tu **parles** anglais ?*

spider
l'**araignée** *f*

spoon
la **cuillère**

sport
le **sport**

square
le **carré**

stairs
l'**escalier** *m*

star
l'**étoile** *f*

station
la gare

stick
coller

Stick it onto the paper.
Colle-le sur le papier.

sticker
l'autocollant *m*

stone
la pierre

stop
arrêter

Stop, that's enough!
Arrête, ça suffit !

story
l'histoire *f*

street
la rue

strong
fort, forte

She's very *strong*.
Elle est très *forte*.

sun
le soleil

supermarket
le supermarché

surprise
la surprise

What a *surprise*!
Quelle *surprise* !

swim
nager

I can *swim*.
Je sais *nager*.

swimming pool
la piscine

table
la **table**

take
prendre
Take a card.
Prends une carte.

talk
parler
You talk too much.
Tu parles trop.

tall
haut, haute
a very tall building
un très haut immeuble

taxi
le **taxi**

tea
le **thé**

teddy bear
le **nounours**

television
la **télévision**

text
envoyer un SMS à
Can you text Lara?
Tu peux envoyer un SMS à Lara ?

text message
le **SMS**

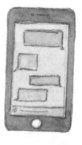

thank you
merci !

think
penser

*What **are** you **thinking** about?*
*À quoi tu **penses** ?*

third
troisième

*the **third** prize*
*le **troisième** prix*

tie
la cravate

tiger
le tigre

tired
fatigué, fatiguée

*I'm **tired**.*
*Je suis **fatigué**.*

toast
le pain grillé

today
aujourd'hui

*It's Monday **today**.*
Aujourd'hui c'est lundi.

together
ensemble

toilet
les toilettes *fpl*

tomato
la tomate

tomorrow
demain

*See you **tomorrow**!*
*À **demain** !*

tooth
la dent

toothbrush
la brosse à dents

a b c d e f g h i j k l m n o p q r s **t** u v w x y z

49

la

toothpaste
le **dentifrice**

tortoise
la **tortue**

towel
la **serviette**

toy
le **jouet**

tractor
le **tracteur**

train
le **train**

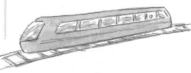

treasure
le **trésor**

tree
l'**arbre** _m_

triangle
le **triangle**

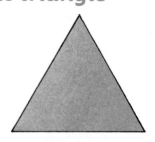

trousers
le **pantalon**

T-shirt
le **tee-shirt**

twin
le **jumeau** _m_/
la **jumelle** _f_

vet
le **vétérinaire** _m_/
la **vétérinaire** _f_

umbrella
le **parapluie**

vanilla
la **vanille**

vanilla ice cream
la glace à la **vanille**

video game
le **jeu vidéo**

uniform
l'**uniforme** _m_

vegetable
le **légume**

visit
visiter

We're going to **visit** the castle.
Nous allons **visiter** le château.

up
en haut

The cat is **up** on the roof.
Le chat est **en haut** sur le toit.

very
très

**very** small
**très** petit

upstairs
en haut

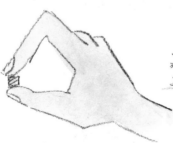

wait
attendre
Wait for me!
Attends-moi !

wake up
se réveiller
Wake up!
Réveille-toi !

walk
marcher
He walks fast.
Il marche vite.

wall
le mur
There are pictures on the wall.
Il y a des images au mur.

want
vouloir
Do you want some cake?
Tu veux du gâteau ?

warm
chaud, chaude
warm water
l'eau chaude

wash
se laver
Wash your hands!
Lave-toi les mains !

watch
la montre

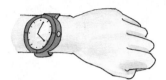

water
l'eau f

wave
la vague

wear
porter
He's wearing a hat.
Il porte un chapeau.

webcam
la webcam

website
le site web

week
la semaine

*I play football every **week**.*
*Je joue au football chaque **semaine**.*

weekend
le week-end

*I go fishing at the **weekend**.*
*Je fais la pêche le **week-end**.*

welcome
bienvenue !

well
bien

*She played **well**.*
*Elle a **bien** joué.*

wet
mouillé, mouillée

wheelchair
le fauteuil roulant

white
blanc, blanche

*I'm wearing a **white** shirt.*
*Je porte une chemise **blanche**.*

wild
sauvage

*a **wild** animal*
*un animal **sauvage***

win
gagner

*I always **win**.*
*Je **gagne** tout le temps.*

wind
le vent

window
la fenêtre

winner
le **gagnant** m/
la **gagnante** f

with
avec

*Come **with** me.*
*Viens **avec** moi.*

without
sans

***without** a coat*
***sans** manteau*

wolf
le **loup**

woman
la **femme**

word
le **mot**

work
travailler

*She **works** in a bank.*
*Elle **travaille** dans une banque.*

world
le **monde**

write
écrire

*I'm **writing** to my friend.*
*J'**écris** à mon ami.*

wrong
faux, fausse

*That answer is **wrong**.*
*Cette réponse est **fausse**.*

X-ray
la **radio**

year
l'**an** m

*I'm seven **years** old.*
*J'ai sept **ans**.*

zebra
le **zèbre**

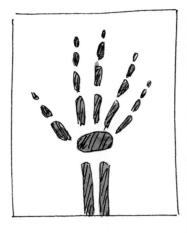

yellow
jaune

zoo
le **zoo**

xylophone
le **xylophone**

yesterday
hier

*I was late **yesterday**.*
*J'étais en retard **hier**.*

young
jeune

*The children are **young**.*
Les enfants sont jeunes.

Conversations
Les conversations

Please
S'il te plaît

Hello!
Bonjour !

How are you?
Comment vas-tu ?

I'm fine, and you?
Je vais bien, et toi ?

Thank you
Merci

You're welcome
De rien

What's your name?
Comment tu t'appelles ?

My name's Eve.
Je m'appelle Eve.

Goodbye
Au revoir

Things I like to do
Les choses que j'aime faire

painting
peindre

watching TV
regarder la TV

dancing
danser

riding my bike
faire du vélo

playing games
jouer à des jeux

singing
chanter

playing football
jouer au foot

reading
lire

swimming
nager

drawing
dessiner

The park
Le parc

sandpit
le bac à sable

swing
la balançoire

climbing frame
la cage à poules

roundabout
le manège

slide
le toboggan

The seaside
Le bord de mer

sea
la mer

bucket and spade
le seau et la pelle

crab
le crabe

starfish
l'étoile de mer *f*

gull
la mouette

rockpool
la flaque d'eau

sand
le sable

61

Vehicles
Les véhicules

tractor
le tracteur

plane
l'avion *m*

fire engine
le camion de pompiers

bike
le vélo

motorbike
la moto

helicopter
l'hélicoptère m

bus
le bus

car
la voiture

ambulance
l'ambulance f

train
le train

Food and drink
La nourriture et les boissons

apple
la pomme

orange
l'orange *f*

banana
la banane

ice cream
la glace

cake
le gâteau

biscuits
les biscuits *mpl*

juice
le jus

milk
le lait

chocolate
le chocolat

bread
le pain

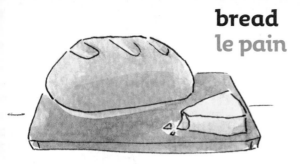

pizza
la pizza

cheese
le fromage

sandwich
le sandwich

crisps
les chips *fpl*

chips
les frites *fpl*

peas
les petits
pois *mpl*

pasta
les pâtes *fpl*

salad
la salade

chicken
le poulet

potatoes
les pommes
de terre *fpl*

carrots
les carottes *fpl*

Clothes
Les vêtements

hat
le chapeau

dress
la robe

T-shirt
le tee-shirt

skirt
la jupe

shoes
les chaussures *fpl*

trainers
les baskets *fpl*

gloves
les gants *mpl*

sweatshirt
le sweat-shir

coat
le manteau

scarf
l'écharpe *f*

jeans
le jean

socks
les chaussettes *fpl*

Parts of the body
Le corps

finger
le doigt

ear
l'oreille *f*

eye
l'œil *m*

arm
le bras

tummy
le ventre

hand
la main

toe
l'orteil *m*

leg
la jambe

hair
les cheveux *mpl*

nose
le nez

head
la tête

cheek
la joue

mouth
la bouche

lip
la lèvre

knee
le genou

foot
le pied

Family
La famille

aunt
la tante

grandma
la grand-mère

sister
la sœur

mum
maman

dad
papa

cousin
le cousin /
la cousine

uncle
l'oncle *m*

grandad
le grand-père

brother
le frère

Animals
Les animaux

cat
le chat

goldfish
le poisson rouge

hamster
le hamster

rabbit
le lapin

dog
le chien

budgie
la perruche

donkey
l'âne *m*

chicken
le poulet

duck
le canard

horse
le cheval

cow
la vache

sheep
le mouton

71

Wild animals
Les animaux sauvages

kangaroo
le kangourou

monkey
le singe

lion
le lion

giraffe
la girafe

hippo
l'hippopotame *m*

crocodile
le crocodile

snake
le serpent

penguin
le manchot

tiger
le tigre

elephant
l'éléphant *m*

Mythical creatures
Les créatures légendaires

alien
l'extraterrestre *m*

giant
le géant

dragon
le dragon

ghost
le fantôme

monster
le monstre

fairy
la fée

mermaid
la sirène

unicorn
la licorne

French-English Index

A, a

acheter **buy**

l'adulte *m/f* **adult**

l'agneau *m* (les agneaux) **lamb**

aimer **like, love**

l'aire de jeux *f* **playground**

aller **go**

l'alphabet *m* **alphabet**

l'ambulance *f* **ambulance**

l'ami *m*/l'amie *f* **friend**

l'an *m* **year**

l'animal *m* (les animaux) **animal, pet**

l'anniversaire *m* **birthday**

appeler **call**

l'appli *f* **app**

apporter **bring**

apprendre **learn**

après **after**

l'après-midi *m* **afternoon**

l'araignée *f* **spider**

l'arbre *m* **tree**

l'arc-en-ciel *m* **rainbow**

l'argent *m* **money**

l'argent de poche *m* **pocket money**

arrêter **stop**

s'asseoir **sit**

attendre **wait**

au revoir **goodbye**

aujourd'hui **today**

l'autocollant *m* **sticker**

autre **other**

avant **before**

avec **with**

l'avion *m* **aeroplane, plane**

avoir **have**

avoir besoin de **need**

B, b

la bague **ring**

les baguettes *fpl* **chopsticks**

le bain **bath**

le ballon **ball, balloon**

la banane **banana**

le bateau (les bateaux) **boat**

le bazar **mess**

beaucoup de **many**

le bébé **baby**

le beurre **butter**

bien **well**

bienvenue **welcome**

le bisou **kiss**

blanc, blanche **white**

bleu, bleue **blue**

boire **drink**

la boîte **box**

bon, bonne **good, right**

le bonhomme de neige **snowman**

bonjour **hello**

la botte **boot**

la bouche **mouth**

la bougie **candle**

le bras **arm**

la brosse à dents **toothbrush**

le bruit **noise**

le bus **bus**

C, c

se cacher **hide**

le cadeau (les cadeaux) **present**

le café **coffee**

le calendrier **calendar**

le camion **lorry**

le canapé **sofa**

le canard **duck**

la carotte **carrot**

le carré **square**

la carte **card**

la carte postale **postcard**

la casquette **cap**

le **cercle** **circle**

le **cerf-volant** **kite**

la **chaise** **chair**

la **chambre**
  bedroom

chanter **sing**

le **chapeau** (les
  chapeaux) **hat**

le **chat** **cat**

le **château** (les
  châteaux) **castle**

le **chaton** **kitten**

chaud, chaude
  hot, warm

la **chaussette** **sock**

la **chaussure** **shoe**

la **chemise** **shirt**

la **chenille**
  caterpillar

le **cheval** (les
  chevaux) **horse**

les **cheveux** *mpl*
  hair

la **chèvre** **goat**

le **chien** **dog**

le **chiot** **puppy**

le **chocolat**
  chocolate

le **ciel** **sky**

le **cirque** **circus**

les **ciseaux** *mpl*
  scissors

le **citron** **lemon**

la **classe**
  classroom

la **clé** **key**

le **clown** **clown**

le **cochon d'Inde**
  guinea pig

le **coiffeur** *m/*
  la **coiffeuse** *f*
  hairdresser

la **colle** **glue**

coller **stick**

compter **count**

la **confiture** **jam**

le **corps** **body**

le **costume**
  costume

courir **run**

la **course** **race**

le **couteau** (les
  couteaux) **knife**

la **couverture**
  blanket

la **cravate** **tie**

le **crayon** **pencil**

crier **shout**

la **cuillère** **spoon**

la **cuisine** **kitchen**

cuisiner **cook**

D, d

la **dame** **lady**

**dangereux,
  dangereuse**
  dangerous

danser **dance**

le **dauphin** **dolphin**

de **from, of**

le **déjeuner** **lunch**

demain **tomorrow**

demander à **ask**

la **dent** **tooth**

le **dentifrice**
  toothpaste

se **dépêcher**
  hurry up

le **dessert** **dessert**

le **dessin** **picture**

dessiner **draw**

deuxième **second**

les **devoirs** *mpl*
  homework

le **dictionnaire**
  dictionary

difficile **difficult**

le **dîner** **dinner**

le **dinosaure**
  dinosaur

dire **say**

le **doigt** **finger**

donner **give**

dormir **sleep**

la **douche** **shower**

drôle **funny**

dur, dure **hard**

le **DVD** **DVD**

E, e

l'**eau** *f* **water**

l'**école** *f* **school**

écouter **listen**

écrire **write**

l'**éléphant** *m*
  elephant

en bas **downstairs**

en haut **up,
  upstairs**

en retard **late**

encore une fois
  again

l'enfant *m/f* **child**
ensemble **together**
entendre **hear**
envoyer **send**
envoyer un SMS à
  text
l'escalier *m* **stairs**
l'escargot *m* **snail**
l'espace *m* **space**
et **and**
l'étoile *f* **star**
l'exercice *m* **exercise**

F, f
facile **easy**
faire **do, make**
la famille **family**
fatigué,
  fatiguée **tired**
le fauteuil roulant
  wheelchair
faux, fausse **wrong**
la femme **woman**
la fenêtre **window**
la fête **party**
le feu (les feux) **fire**
les feux d'artifice
  mpl **fireworks**
la figure **face**
la fille **daughter,
  girl**
le fils **son**
la flaque **puddle**
la fleur **flower**
le football **football**
la forêt **forest**
fort, forte **loud,
  strong**

la fourchette **fork**
le frère **brother**
le frigo **fridge**
les frites *fpl* **chips**
froid, froide **cold**
le fromage **cheese**
le fruit **fruit**
la fusée **rocket**

G, g
le gagnant *m/*
  la gagnante *f*
  winner
gagner **win**
le gant **glove**
le garage **garage**
le garçon **boy**
garder **keep**
la gare **station**
le gâteau (les
  gâteaux) **cake**
le genou (les
  genoux) **knee**
les gens *mpl* **people**
gentil, gentille
  kind, nice
la girafe **giraffe**
la glace **ice cream**
le gosse *m/*la gosse
  f **kid**
grand, grande **big**
grandir **grow**
la grenouille **frog**
la guitare **guitar**

H, h
habiter **live**
le hamburger
  burger

le hamster
  hamster
haut, haute **tall**
l'hélicoptère *m*
  helicopter
l'herbe *f* **grass**
le hérisson
  hedgehog
l'heure *f* **hour**
heureux, heureuse
  happy
hier **yesterday**
l'histoire *f* **story**
l'homme *m* **man**
l'hôpital *m* (les
  hôpitaux) **hospital**
l'horloge *f* **clock**

I, i
ici **here**
l'île *f* **island**
l'infirmier
  *m/*l'infirmière *f*
  nurse
l'insecte *m* **insect**
l'Internet *m*
  internet

J, j
la jambe **leg**
le jardin **garden**
jaune **yellow**
le jean **jeans**
le jeu (les jeux)
  game
le jeu vidéo **video
  game**
jeune **young**
joli, jolie **pretty**

jouer **play**

le jouet **toy**

le jour **day**

le journal (les journaux) **newspaper**

le jumeau *m*/la jumelle *f* **twin**

la jupe **skirt**

le jus **juice**

L, l

le lac **lake**

le lait **milk**

la lampe **lamp**

le lapin **rabbit**

se laver **wash**

le légume **vegetable**

lent, lente **slow**

la lettre **letter**

le lion **lion**

lire **read**

le lit **bed**

le livre **book**

le loup **wolf**

la lumière **light**

la lune **moon**

les lunettes *fpl* **glasses**

M, m

le magasin **shop**

le magicien *m*/la magicienne *f* **magician**

le mail **email**

la main **hand**

maintenant **now**

la maison **house**

malade **sick**

la maman **mum**

manger **eat**

le manteau (les manteaux) **coat**

le marché **market**

marcher **walk**

la marionnette **puppet**

le matin **morning**

mauvais, mauvaise **bad**

le médecin *m*/la médecin *f* **doctor**

le médicament **medicine**

même **same**

la mer **sea**

merci **thank you**

la mère **mother**

moins **less**

le mois **month**

le monde **world**

la montagne **mountain**

la montre **watch**

montrer **show**

le mot **word**

la moto **motorbike**

la mouche **fly**

mouillé, mouillée **wet**

le mouton **sheep**

le mur **wall**

la musique **music**

N, n

nager **swim**

la neige **snow**

le nez (les nez) **nose**

noir, noire **black**

le nom **name**

le nounours **teddy bear**

la nourriture **food**

nouveau, nouvelle **new**

le nuage **cloud**

la nuit **night**

le numéro **number**

O, o

l'œil *m* (les yeux) **eye**

l'œuf *m* **egg**

l'oiseau *m* (les oiseaux) **bird**

l'ombre *f* **shadow**

l'orange *f* **orange**

l'ordinateur *m* **computer**

l'oreille *f* **ear**

ouvrir **open**

P, p

la page **page**

le pain **bread**

le pain grillé **toast**

le panier **basket**

le pantalon **trousers**

le papa **dad**

le papier **paper**

le papillon **butterfly**

le **parapluie**
umbrella

le **parc** **park**

pardon **sorry**

les **parents** *mpl*
parents

parler **speak, talk**

les **pâtes** *fpl* **pasta**

la **peau** **skin**

peindre **paint**

penser **think**

perdu, perdue **lost**

le **père** **father**

petit, petite **little**

le **petit déjeuner**
breakfast

les **petits pois** *mpl*
peas

la **photo** **photo**

le **piano** **piano**

la **pièce** **room**

la **pierre** **stone**

le **pique-nique**
picnic

le **pirate** **pirate**

la **piscine**
swimming pool

la **pizza** **pizza**

la **plage** **beach**

la **plante** **plant**

plein, pleine **full**

pleurer **cry**

la **pluie** **rain**

la **plume** **feather**

plus de **more**

la **poche** **pocket**

le **poisson** **fish**

le **poisson rouge**
goldfish

le **policier** *m/*
la **policière** *f*
police officer

la **pomme** **apple**

la **pomme de terre**
potato

le **poney** **pony**

le **pont** **bridge**

le **portable** **laptop,**
mobile

le **portail** **gate**

la **porte** **door**

porter **wear**

le **poulet** **chicken**

la **poupée** **doll**

la **poussette**
pushchair

préféré, préférée
favourite

premier, première
first

prendre **take**

prêt, prête **ready**

le **prince** **prince**

la **princesse**
princess

prochain,
prochaine **next**

propre **clean**

le **puzzle** **jigsaw**

le **pyjama** **pyjamas**

R, r

la **radio** **radio,**
X-ray

les **raisins** *mpl*
grapes

rapide **quick**

regarder **look**

la **reine** **queen**

rencontrer **meet**

le **repas** **meal**

le **restaurant**
restaurant

le **rêve** **dream**

se **réveiller** **wake**
up

riche **rich**

rire **laugh**

la **rivière** **river**

le **riz** **rice**

la **robe** **dress**

le **robot** **robot**

le **roi** **king**

rouge **red**

la **route** **road**

le **ruban** **ribbon**

la **rue** **street**

S, s

le **sable** **sand**

le **sac** **bag**

sale **dirty**

le **sandwich**
sandwich

sans **without**

sauter **jump**

sauvage **wild**

savoir **know**

le **savon** **soap**

le **seau** (les **seaux**)
bucket

le **selfie** **selfie**

la **semaine** **week**

sentir **smell**

le **serpent** **snake**
serrer dans ses bras **hug**
la **serviette** **towel**
le **short** **shorts**
le **singe** **monkey**
le **site web** **website**
le **SMS** **text message**
la **sœur** **sister**
le **soir** **evening**
le **soleil** **sun**
la **soupe** **soup**
le **sourire** **smile**
la **souris** **mouse**
le **sport** **sport**
le **stylo** **pen**
le **supermarché** **supermarket**
la **surprise** **surprise**

T, t
la **table** **table**
le **tambour** **drum**
la **tasse** **cup**
le **taxi** **taxi**
le **tee-shirt** **T-shirt**
le **téléphone** **phone**
la **télévision** **television**
la **Terre** **Earth**

la **terre** **ground**
la **tête** **head**
le **thé** **tea**
le **tigre** **tiger**
les **toilettes** *fpl* **toilet**
la **tomate** **tomato**
la **tortue** **tortoise**
tout, toute (tous) **every**
le **tracteur** **tractor**
le **train** **train**
tranquille **quiet**
le **travail** **job**
travailler **work**
très **very**
le **trésor** **treasure**
le **triangle** **triangle**
triste **sad**
troisième **third**
trouver **find**

U, u
l'**uniforme** *m* **uniform**

V, v
les **vacances** *fpl* **holiday**
la **vache** **cow**
la **vague** **wave**
la **vanille** **vanilla**
le **vélo** **bicycle**

venir **come**
le **vent** **wind**
le **verre** **glass**
la **veste** **jacket**
les **vêtements** *mpl* **clothes**
le **vétérinaire** *m*/la **vétérinaire** *f* **vet**
la **viande** **meat**
vide **empty**
vieux, vieille **old**
visiter **visit**
vite **fast**
voir **see**
le **voisin** *m*/ la **voisine** *f* **neighbour**
la **voiture** **car**
vouloir **want**

W, w
la **webcam** **webcam**
le **week-end** **weekend**

X, x
le **xylophone** **xylophone**

Z, z
le **zèbre** **zebra**
le **zoo** **zoo**